AC/DC
ANTHOLOGY

AMSCO PUBLICATIONS
NEW YORK/LONDON/SYDNEY

Cover photography by George DeSota/LFI

This book Copyright © 1991 by Amsco Publications,
A Division of Music Sales Corporation, New York, NY.

Exclusive Distributors:
Music Sales Corporation
257 Park Avenue South, New York, NY 10010 USA
Music Sales Limited
8/9 Frith Street, London W1V 5TZ England
Music Sales Pty. Limited
120 Rothschild Street, Rosebery, Sydney, NSW 2018, Australia

Order No. AM 85564
US International Standard Book Number: 0.8256.1316.7

Printed in the United States of America by
Vicks Lithograph and Printing Corporation

LEGEND OF MUSICAL SYMBOLS

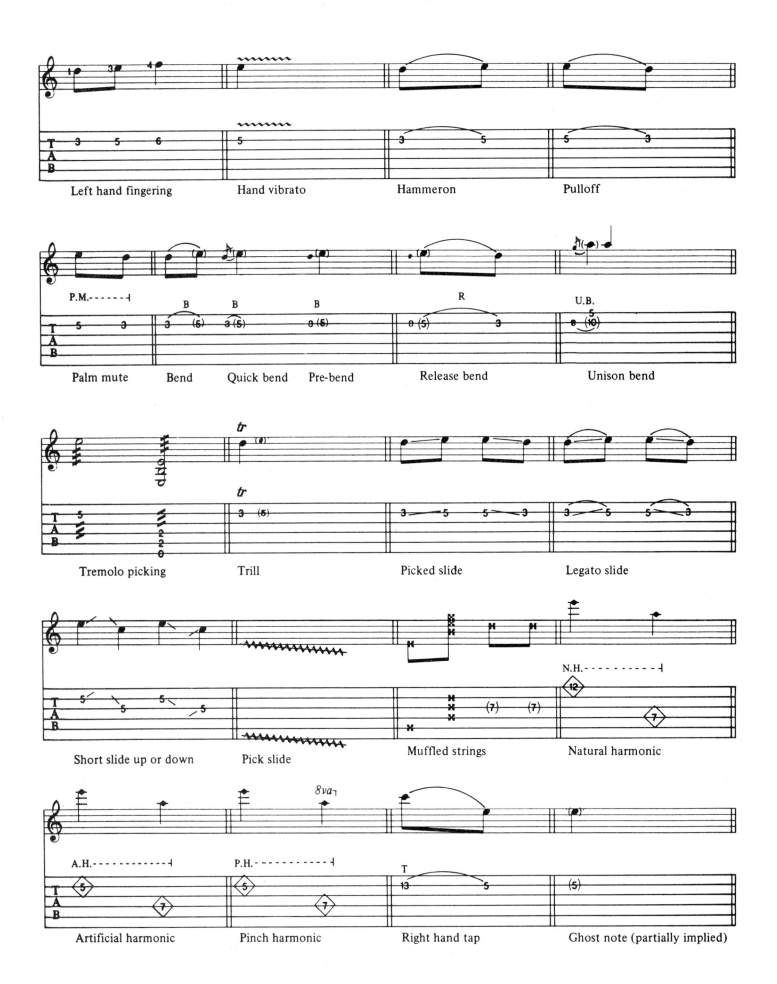

For Those About To Rock
(We Salute You)

Young/Young/Johnson

6

10

Back In Black

Angus Young/Malcolm Young/Brian Johnson

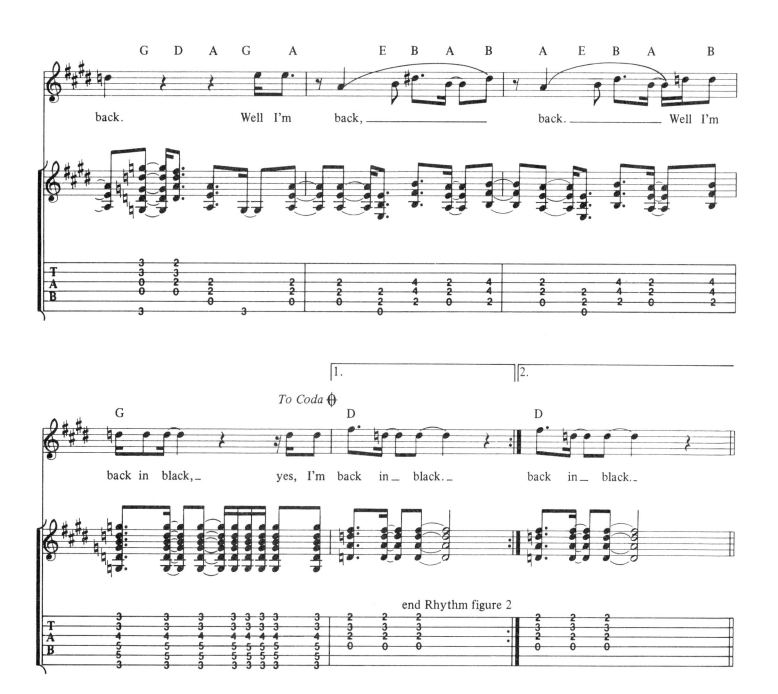

Rhythm figure 3

end Rhythm figure 3

with Rhythm figure 3 (3 times)

Additional Lyrics

2. Back in the back of a Cadillac
   Number one with a bullet, I'm a power pack.
   Yes, I'm in a bang with the gang,
   They gotta catch me if they want me to hang.
   'Cause I'm back on the track, and I'm beatin' the flack
   Nobody's gonna get me on another rap.
   So, look at me now, I'm just makin' my play
   Don't try to push your luck, just get outta my way.

Let Me Put My Love Into You

Angus Young / Malcolm Young / Brian Johnson

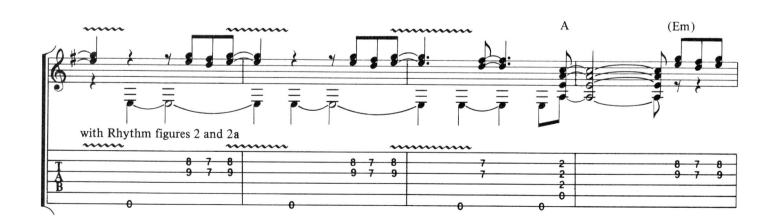

Fly - in' on a free __ flight, driv - in' all __ night With my ma - chin - er - y, __

A5

Rhythm figure 3
with Rhythm figure 1

(Em)

__ 'Cause I, I got the pow - er an - y hour, __

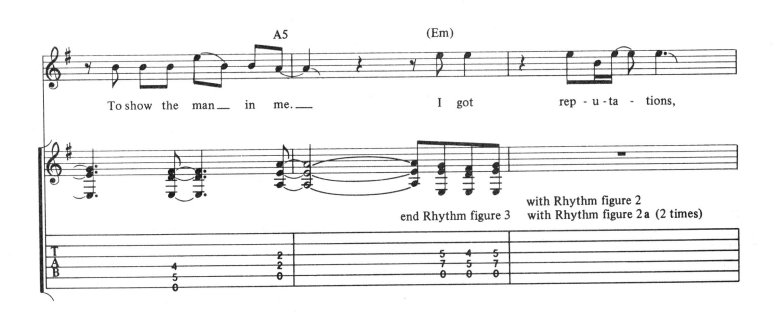

A5 (Em)

To show the man __ in me. __ I got rep - u - ta - tions,

end Rhythm figure 3

with Rhythm figure 2
with Rhythm figure 2 a (2 times)

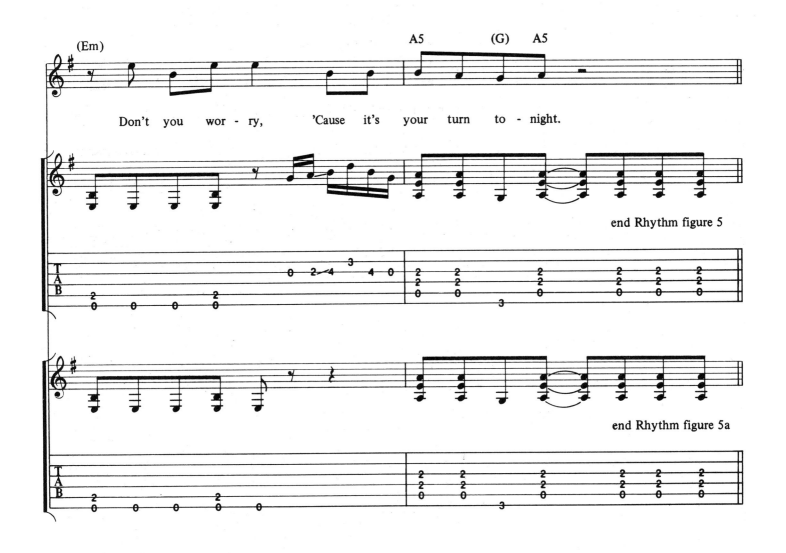

Don't you wor - ry, 'Cause it's your turn to - night.

end Rhythm figure 5

end Rhythm figure 5a

Let me put my love in - to you ___ babe, Let me put my love on the line. ___

Rhythm figure 6

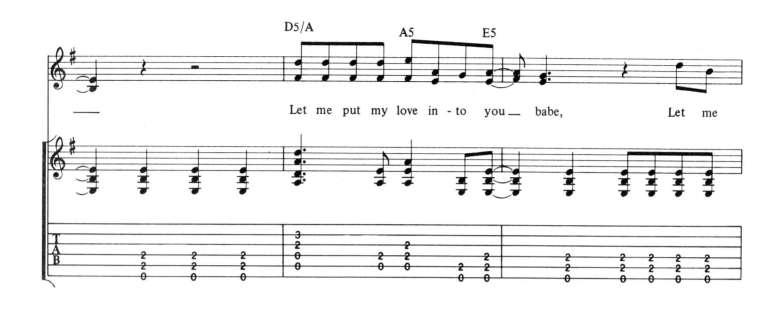

Let me put my love in-to you_ babe, Let me

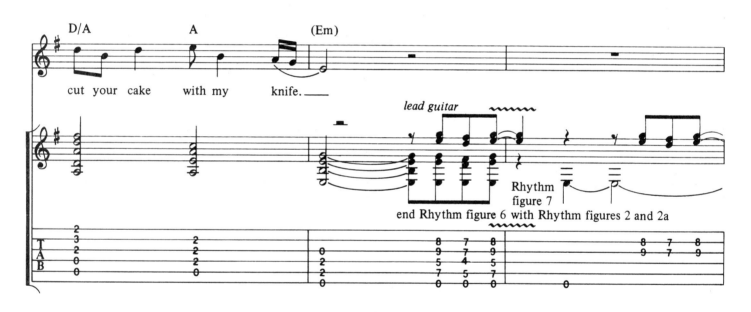

cut your cake with my knife._

lead guitar

Rhythm figure 7

end Rhythm figure 6 with Rhythm figures 2 and 2a

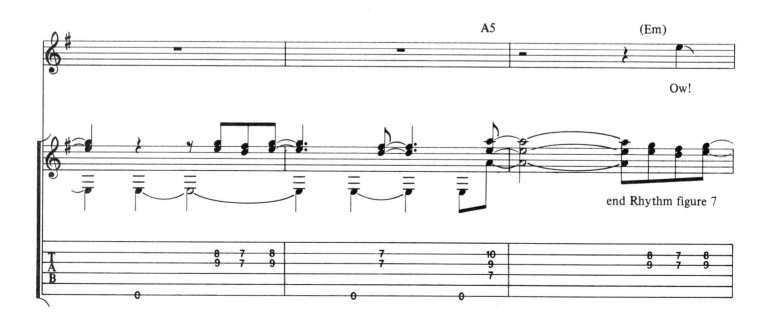

Ow!

end Rhythm figure 7

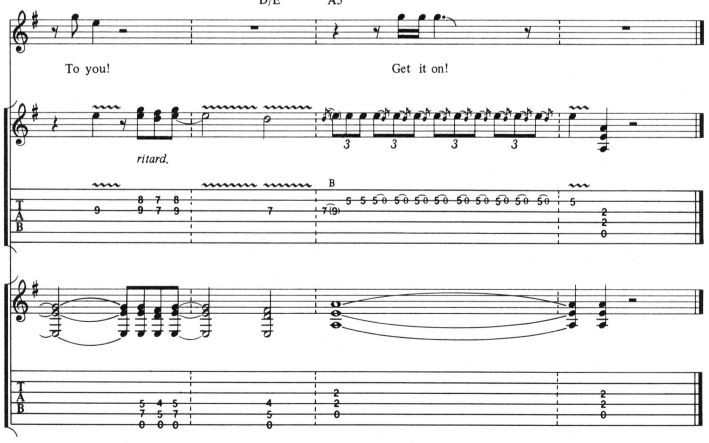

You Shook Me All Night Long

Angus Young/Malcolm Young/Brian Johnson

34

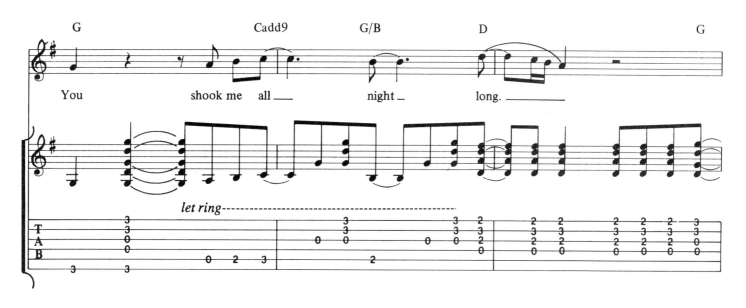

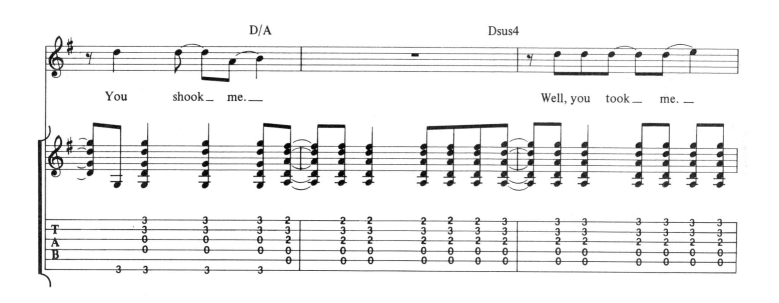

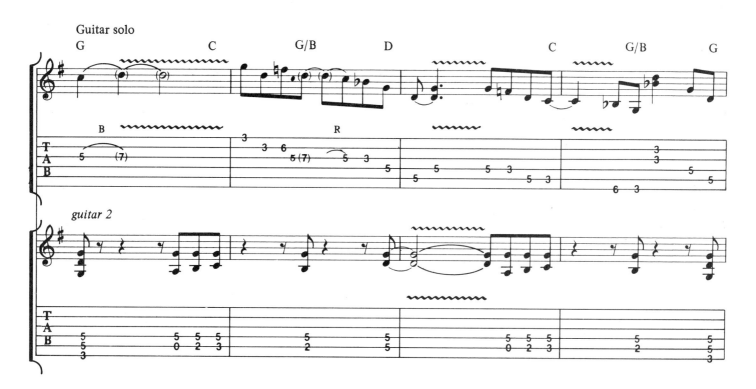

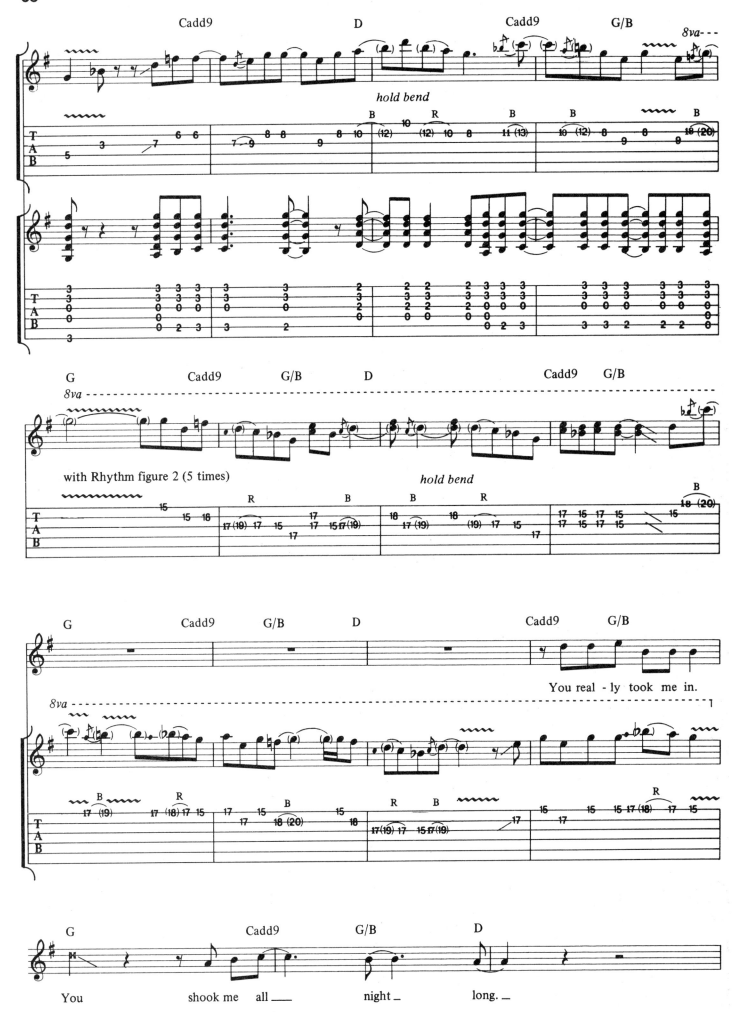

Love At First Feel

Malcolm Young / Angus Young / Bon Scott

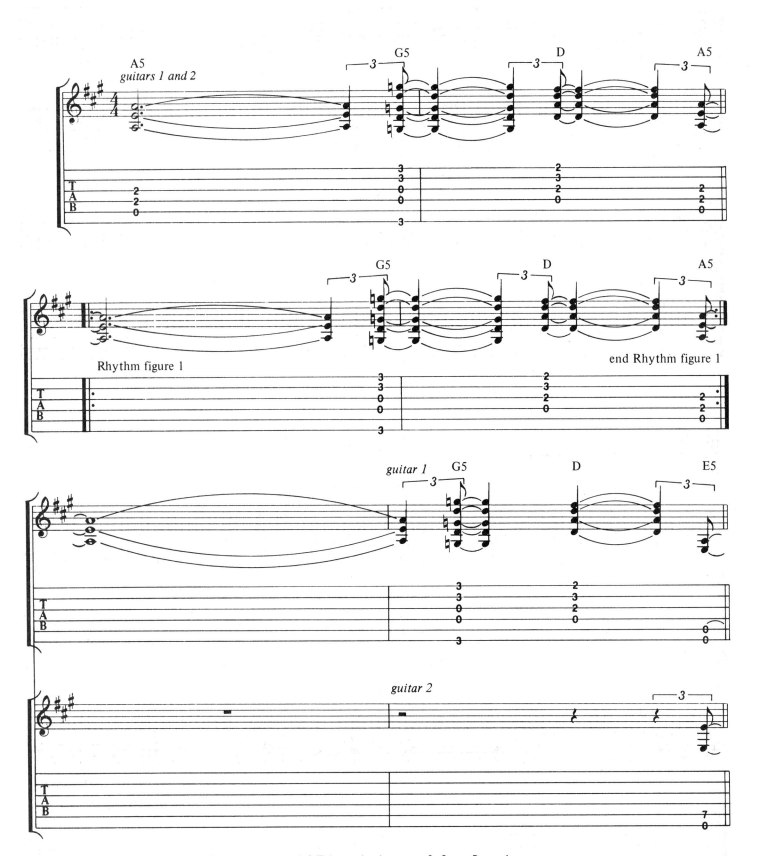

1. You nev-er told_ me_ where you came from,
2. *See additional lyrics*

Rhythm figure 2

Rhythm figure 2a

You nev-er told_ me your name,_

end Rhythm figure 2

end Rhythm figure 2a

40

Additional Lyrics

2. They told me it was disgustin,
   They told me it was a sin,
   They saw me knocking on your front door,
   Saw me smile when you let me in.
   You and me, baby, we's all alone.
   Let's get something goin', while your mom and dad ain't home.

Ride On

Malcolm Young / Angus Young / Bon Scott

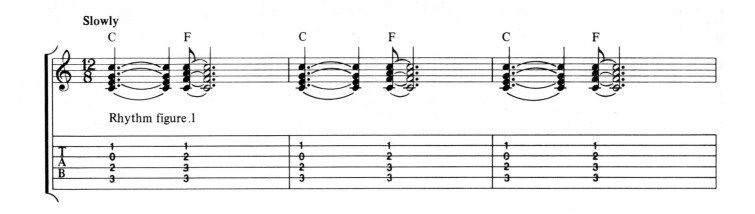

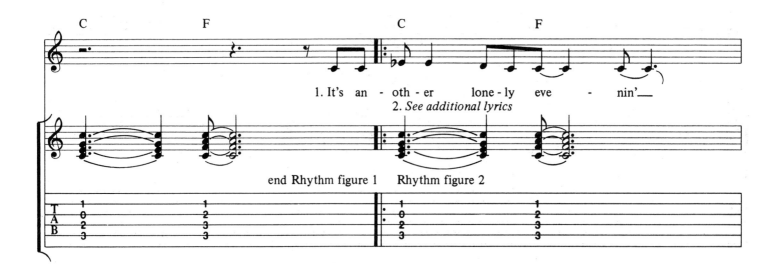

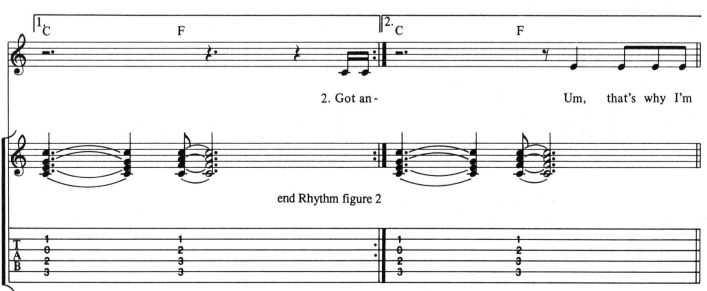

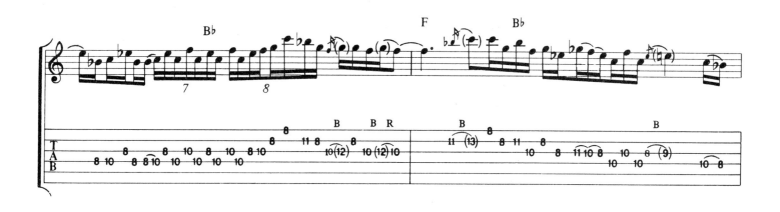

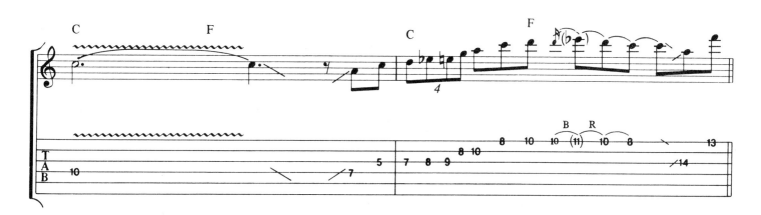

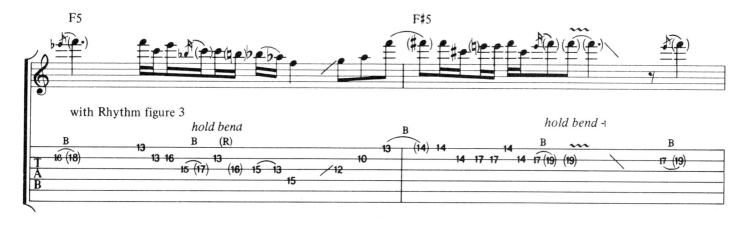

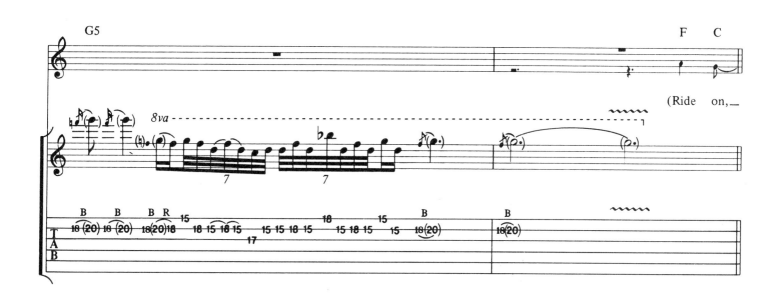

Additional Lyrics

2. Got another empty bottle,
   And another empty bed,
   Ain't too young to admit it,
   And I'm not too old to lie,
   I'm just another empty head.

Squealer

Malcolm Young/Angus Young/Bon Scott

60

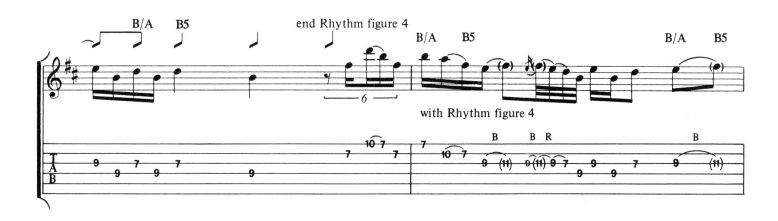

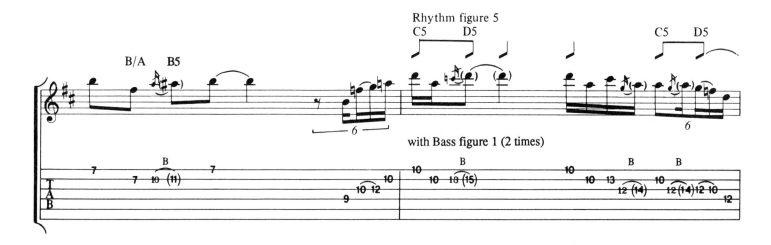

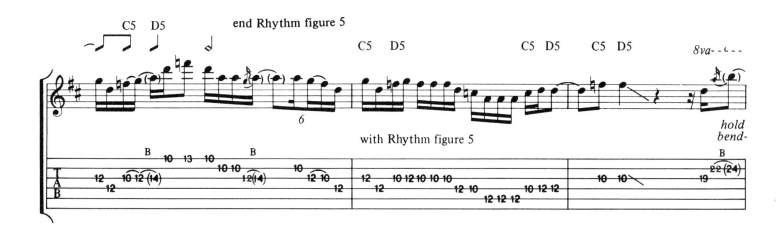

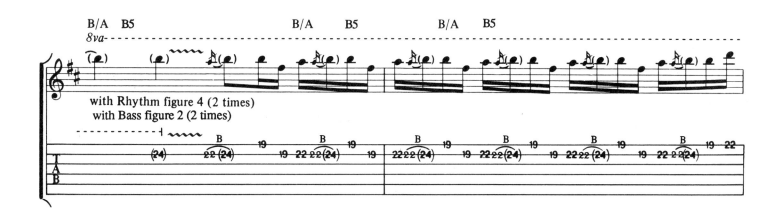

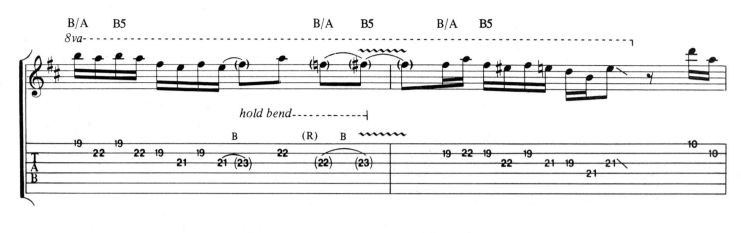

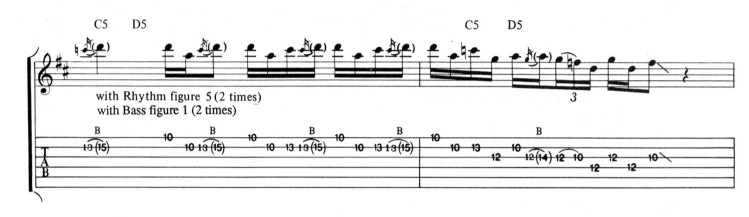

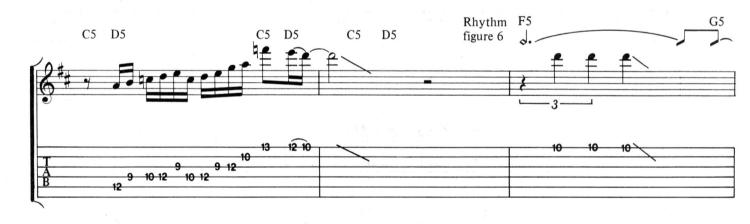

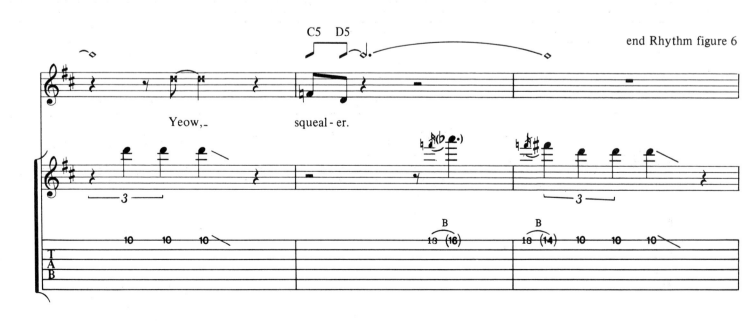

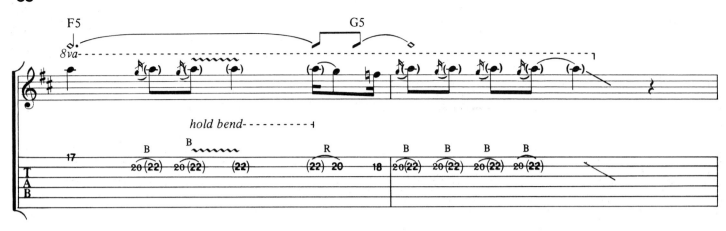

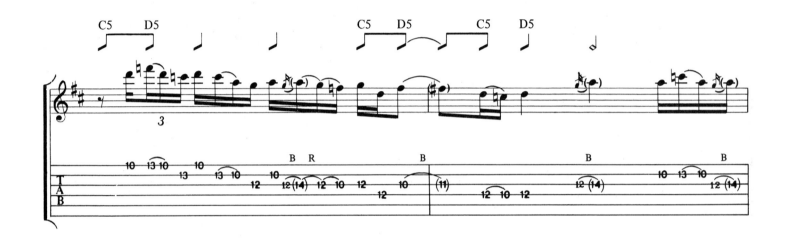

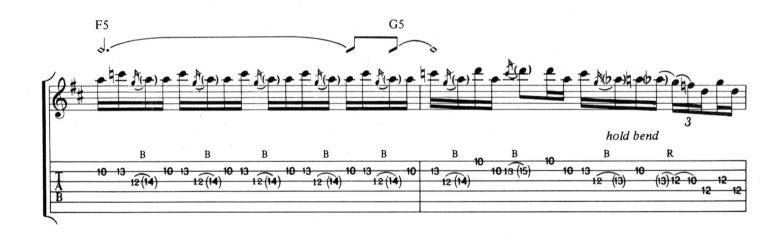

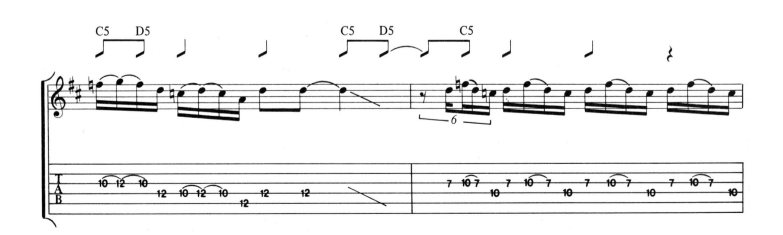

Shake Your Foundations

Young/Young/Johnson

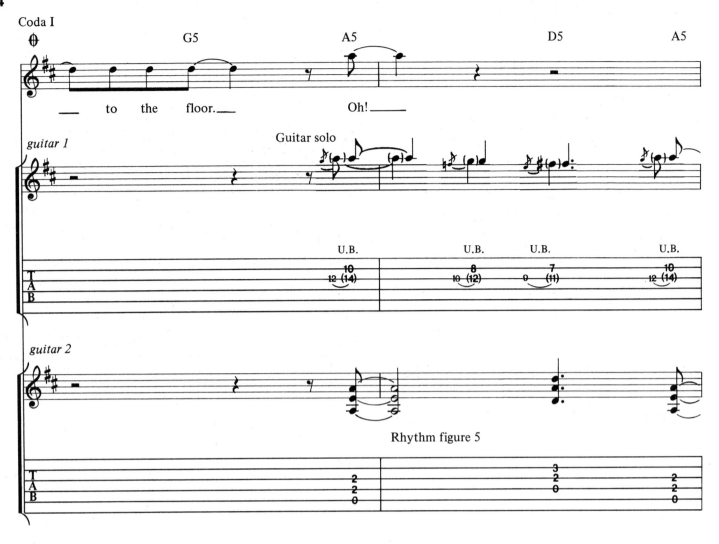

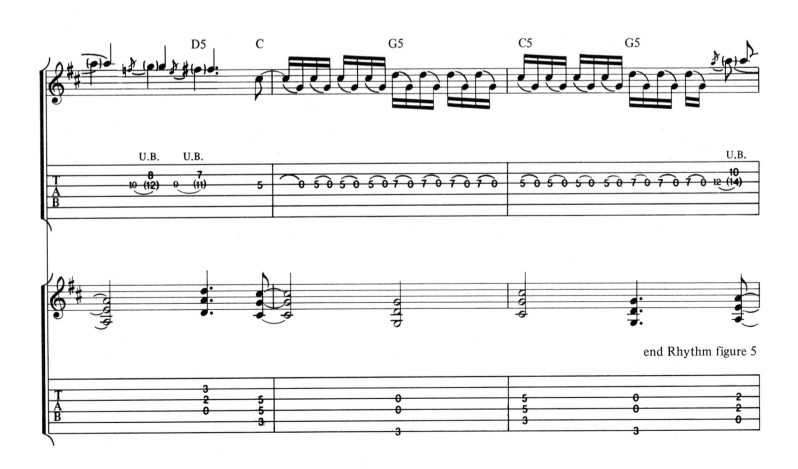

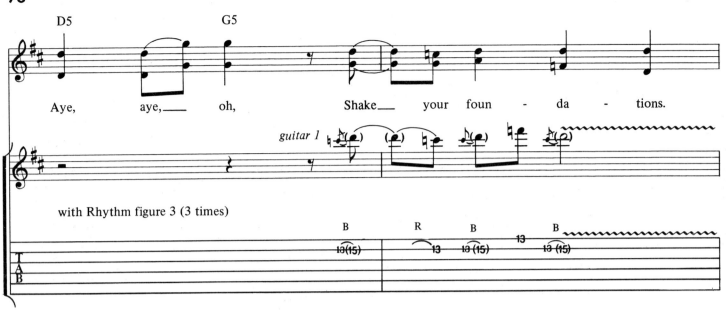

Girls Got Rhythm

Ronald Scott/Angus Young/Malcolm Young

with Rhythm figures 1 and 1a (8 times)

round the world,
2. *See additional lyrics*

I've seen a mil-lion girls.___

Ain't a - one of them got,___ what my

la - dy she's got.___ She's steal-ing the spot - light,___

knocks me off my_ feet._ She's e - nough to start a land - slide,

just a - walk - in' down the street. Wear - in'

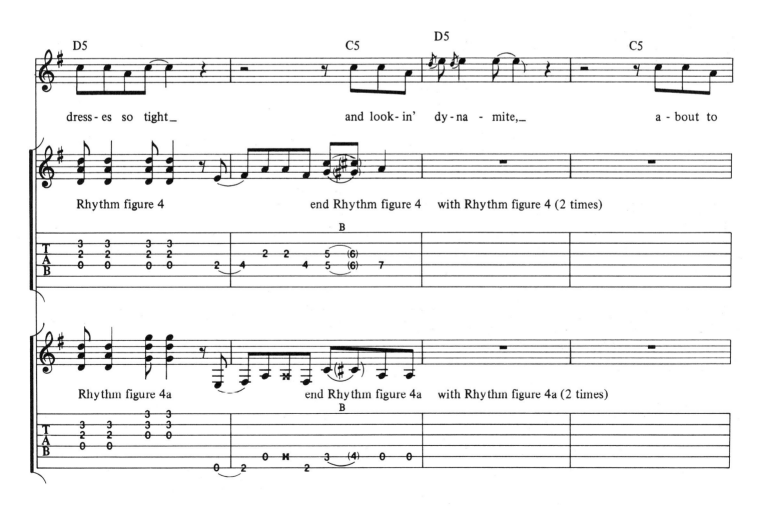

dress - es so tight_ and look - in' dy - na - mite,_ a - bout to

2. Guitar solo

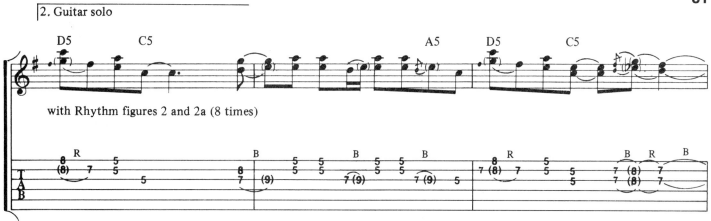

with Rhythm figures 2 and 2a (8 times)

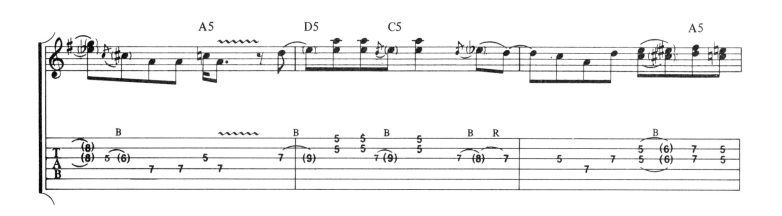

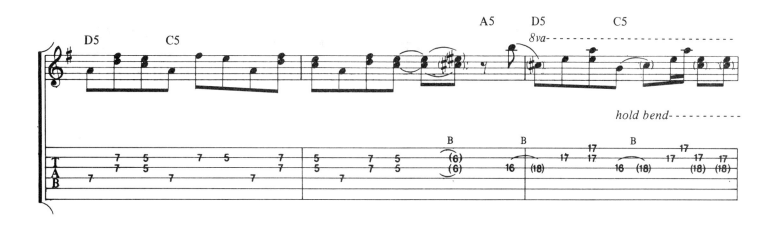

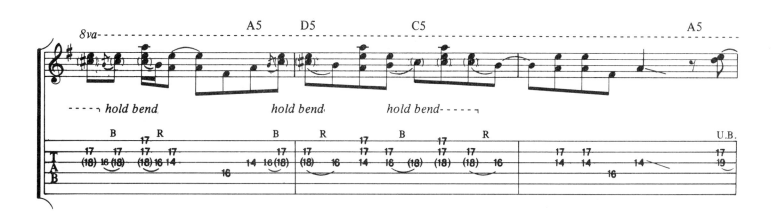

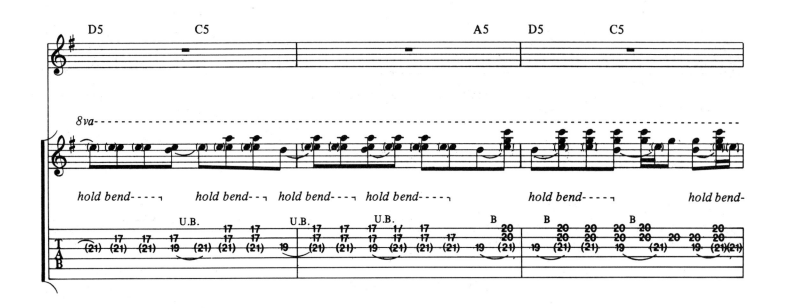

with Rhythm figures 4 and 4a (3 times)

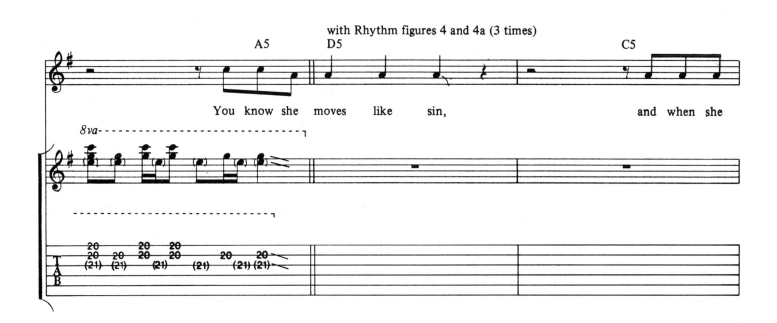

You know she moves like sin, and when she

lets me in It's like a liq - uid love.

with Rhythm figures 5 and 5a

with Rhythm figures 2 and 2a

No doubt a - bout it, can't live with-out it. The girl's got a - rhy - thm.

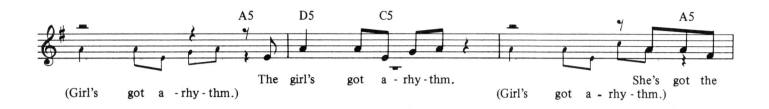

The girl's got a-rhy-thm. (Girl's got a-rhy-thm.) She's got the

(Girl's got a-rhy-thm.)

back seat a-rhy-thm. (Back seat a-rhy-thm.) The girl's got a-rhy-thm.

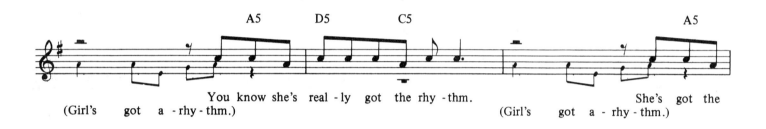

You know she's real-ly got the rhy-thm. She's got the (Girl's got a-rhy-thm.) (Girl's got a-rhy-thm.)

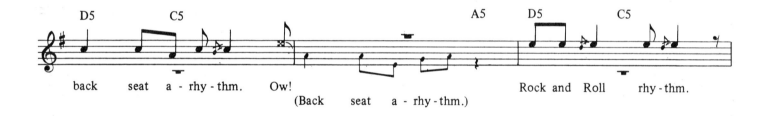

back seat a-rhy-thm. Ow! (Back seat a-rhy-thm.) Rock and Roll rhy-thm.

with Rhythm figures 3 and 3a

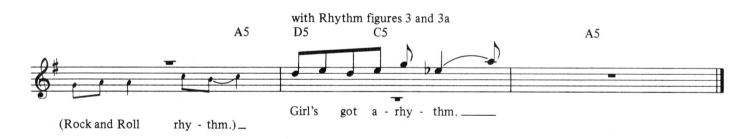

Girl's got a-rhy-thm. (Rock and Roll rhy-thm.)

Additional Lyrics

2. She's like a lethal brand, too much for any man.
She gives me first degree, she really satisfies me.
Loves me till I'm legless, achin' and sore.
Enough to stop a freight train or start the third world war.
You know I'm losin' sleep but I'm in too deep,
Like a body needs blood.

Highway To Hell

Ronald Scott/Angus Young/Malcolm Young

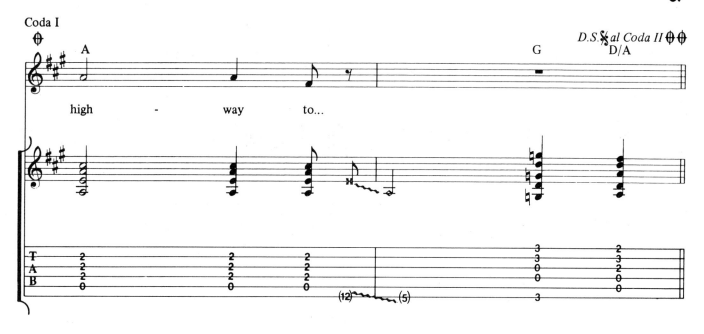

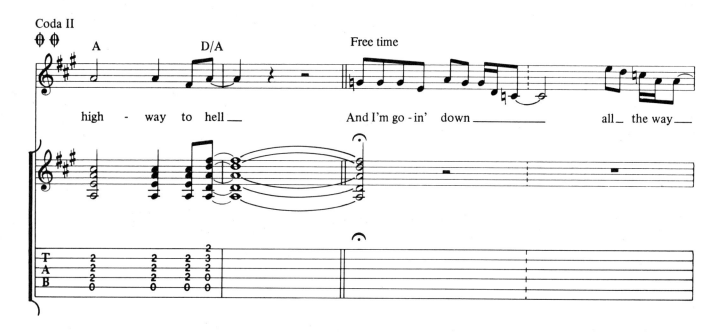

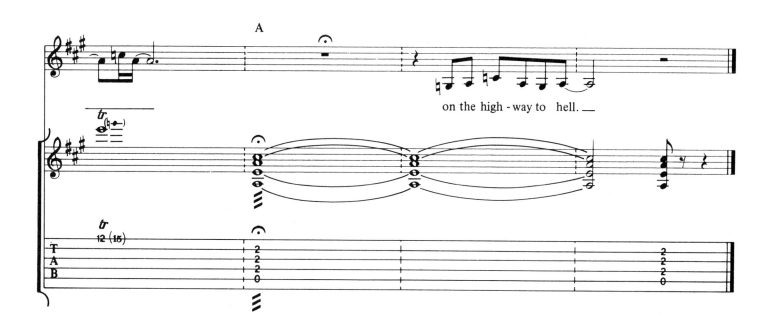

Night Prowler

Ronald Scott/Angus Young/Malcolm Young

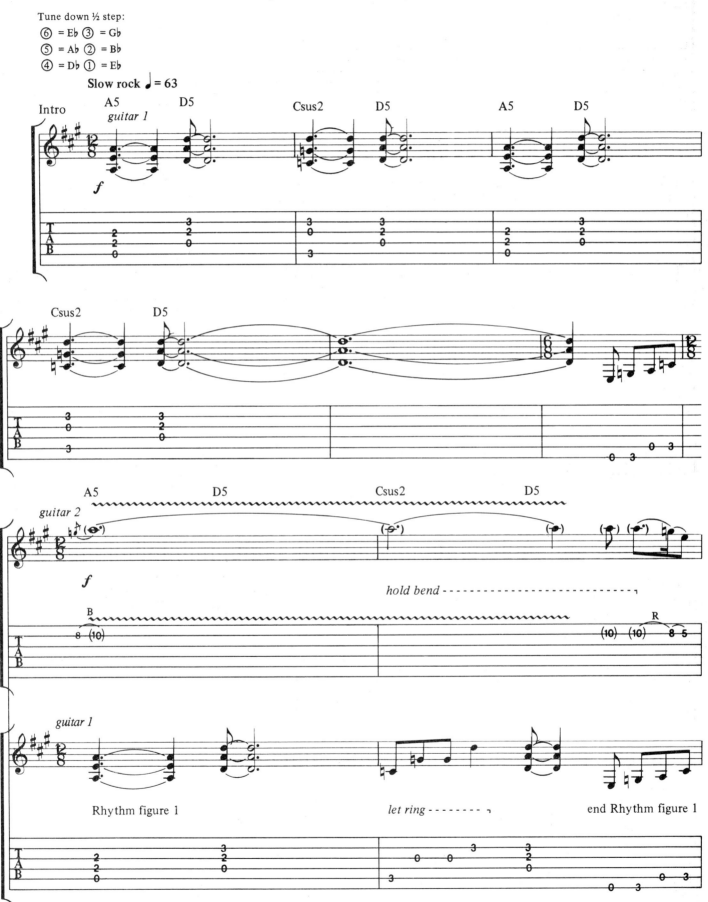

night   prowl - er, ___   when you   shut out   the light.
(Night   prowl - er. ___)

Guitar solo

hold bend -
with Rhythm figure 1 (3½ times)

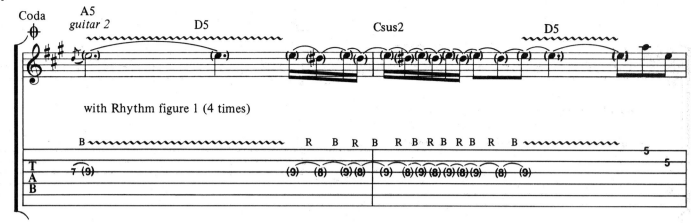

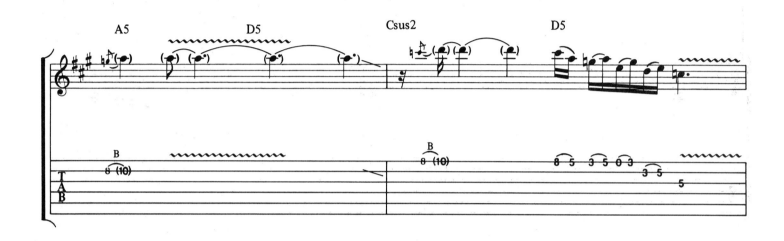

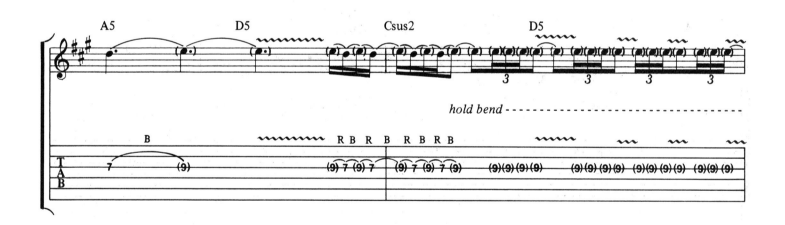

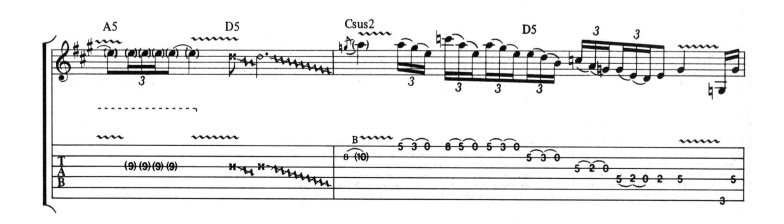

with Rhythm figure 1 (1½ times)

D.S. al Coda II

I'm   your

guitar 1

Shot Down In Flames

Ronald Scott/Angus Young/Malcolm Young

flames.

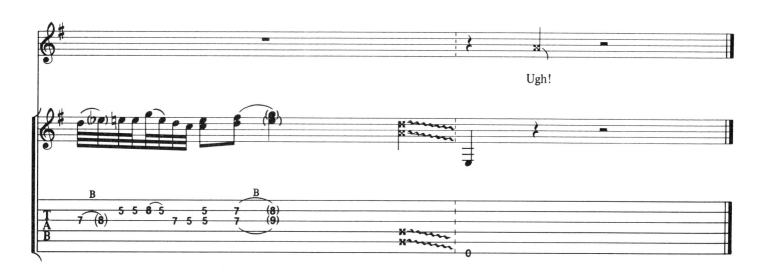

Ugh!

Additional Lyrics

2. Singles bar,
   Got my eye on a honey,
   Hangin' out everywhere.
   She might want my money,
   I really don't care, no!
   Say baby, you're driving me crazy,
   Laying it out on the line.
   When a guy with a chip on his shoulder says,
   "Don't sit buddy, she's mine."

Thunderstruck
Angus Young/Malcolm Young

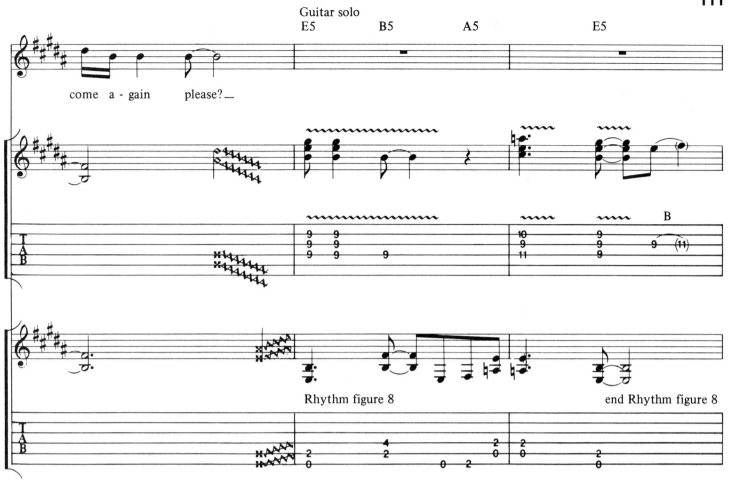

come a - gain please? —

Guitar solo
E5   B5   A5   E5

Rhythm figure 8   end Rhythm figure 8

B

with Rhythm figure 8 (3 times)

B5   A5   E5

B

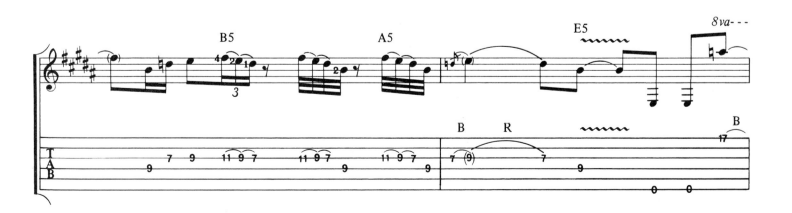

B5   A5   E5   8va- - -

B   R   B

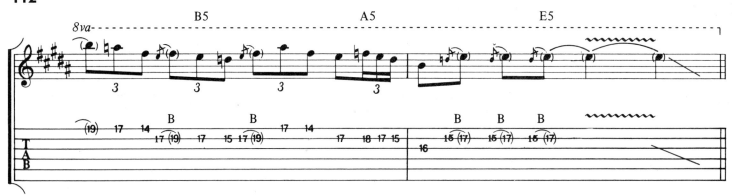

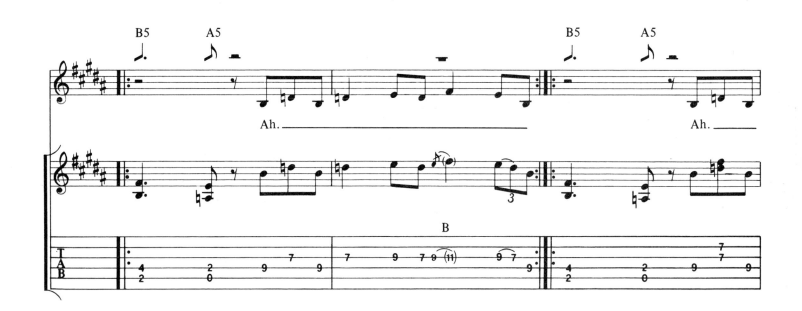

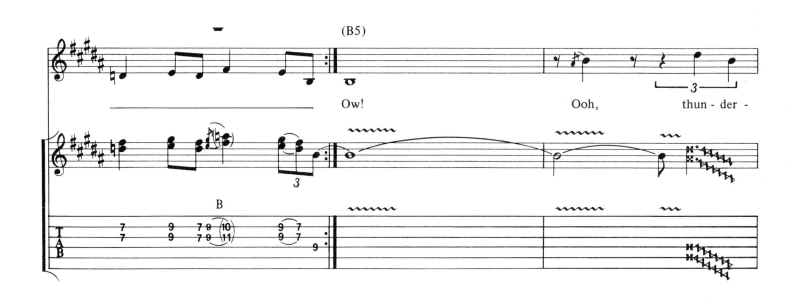

Shoot To Thrill

Angus Young/Malcolm Young/Brian Johnson

Pull it, pull it, pull the trig - ger. _____

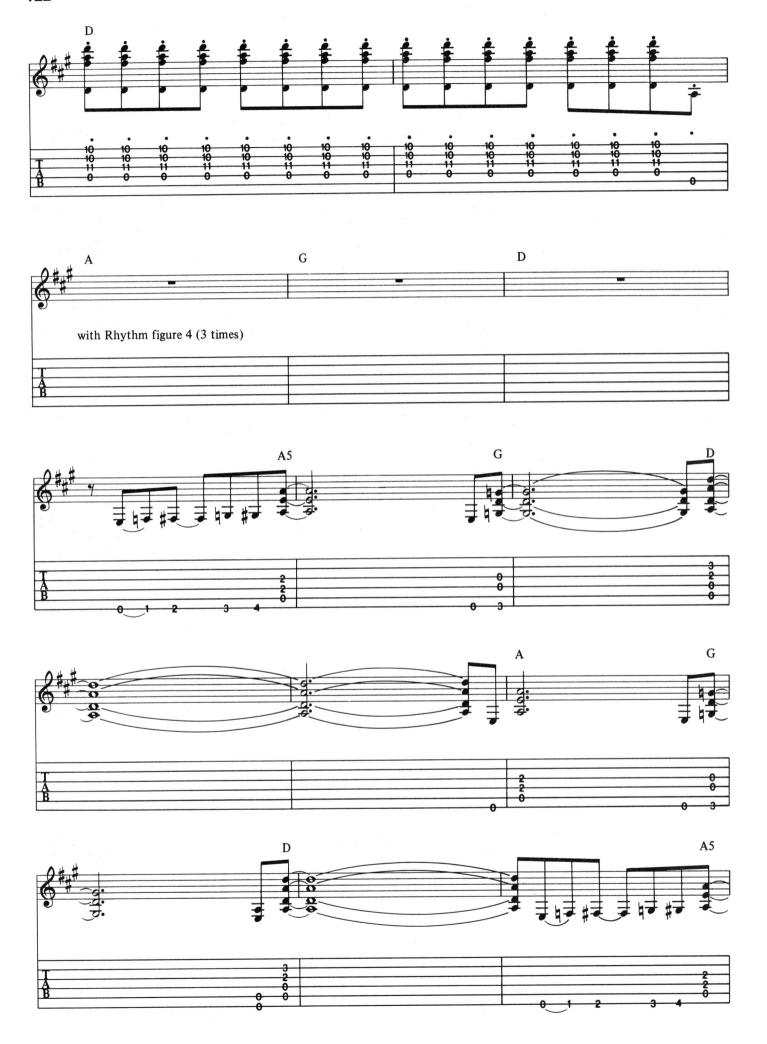

with Rhythm figure 4 (3 times)

Additional Lyrics

2. I'm like evil; I get under your skin,
   Just like a bomb that's ready to blow.
   'Cause I'm illegal; I got everything
   That all you women might need to know.
   I'm gonna take you down,
   Down, down, down.
   So don't you fool around,
   I'm gonna pull it, pull it, pull the trigger.

The Razors Edge

Angus Young / Malcolm Young

Rhythm figure 1

with simile rhythm (14 bars)

end Rhythm figure 1

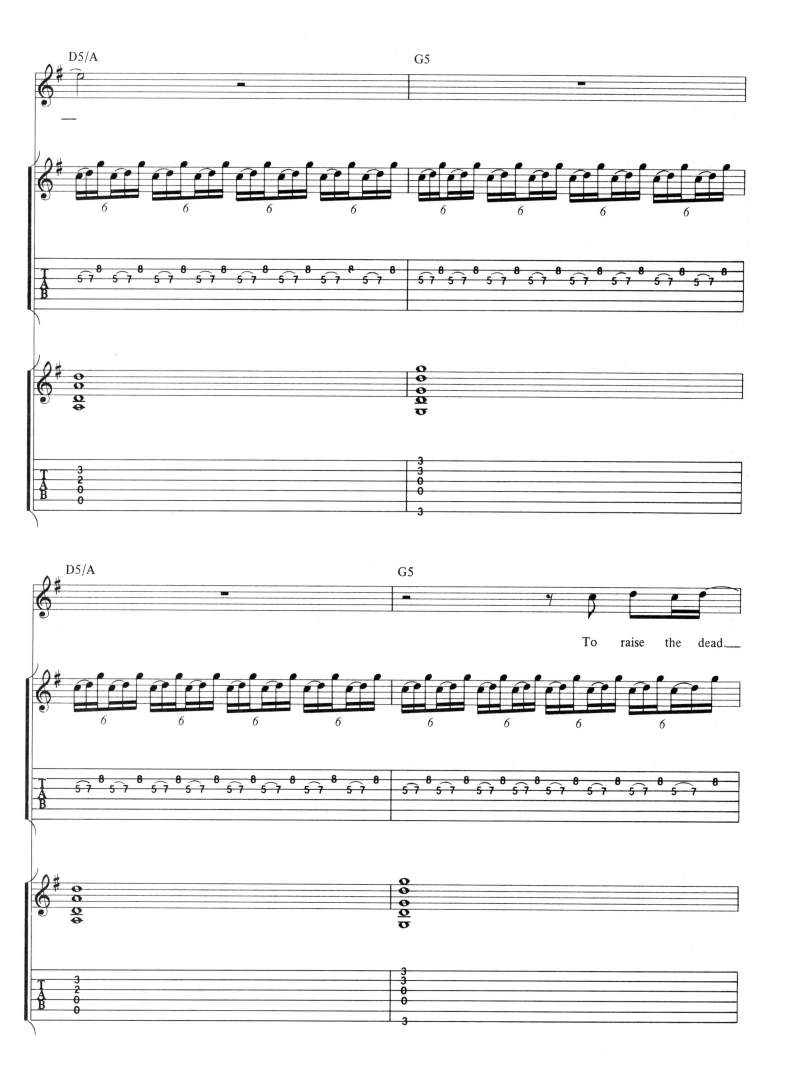

To raise the dead.__

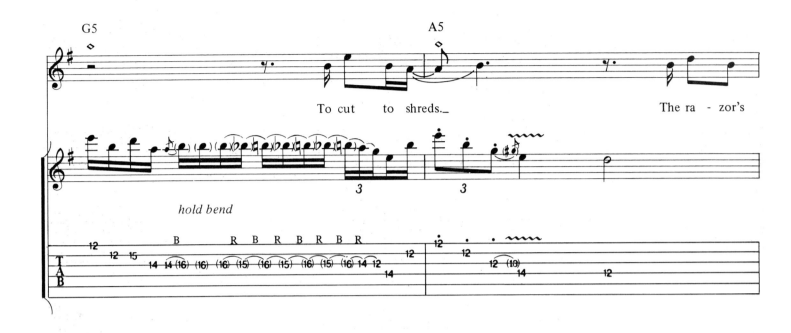

To cut to shreds.___ The ra - zor's

edge. _____ But the ra - zor's edge,___

with Rhythm figure 3 (2 times)

Whoa, the ra - zor's edge!___

But you could cut to shreds,_____

Got-ta ra - zor's edge,_____

What a ra - zor's edge!__

Moneytalks

Angus Young/Malcolm Young

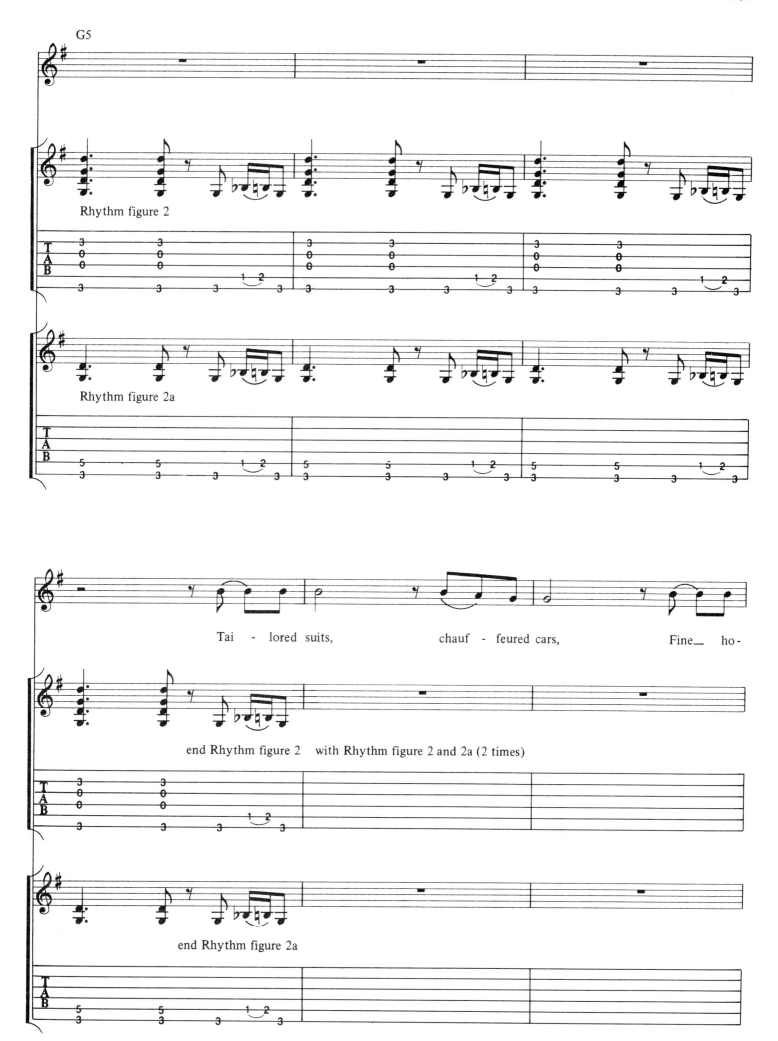

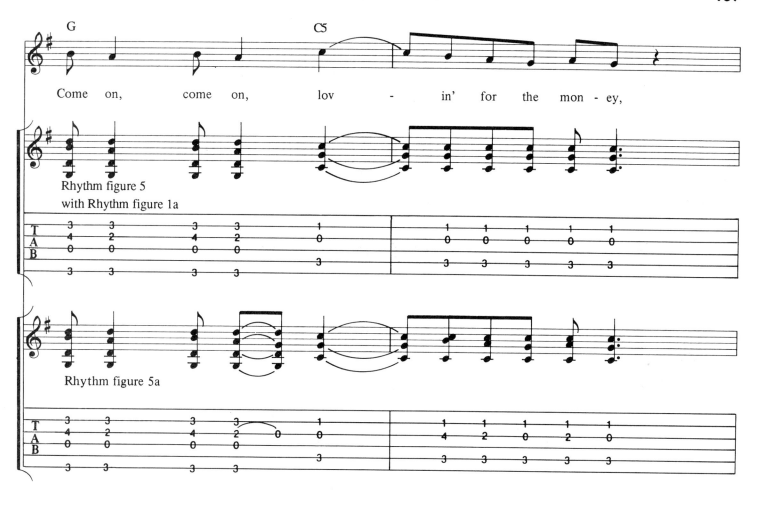

Come on, come on, lov - in' for the mon - ey,

Rhythm figure 5
with Rhythm figure 1a

Rhythm figure 5a

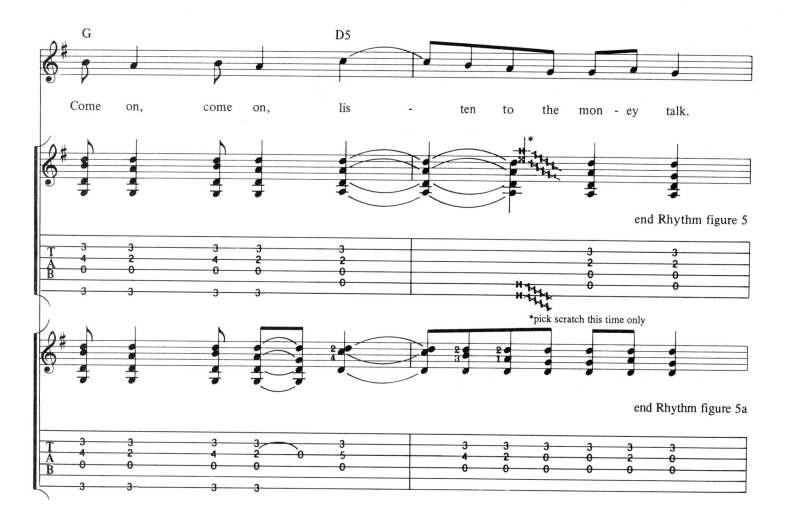

Come on, come on, lis - ten to the mon - ey talk.

end Rhythm figure 5

*pick scratch this time only

end Rhythm figure 5a

with Rhythm figures 1a, 5 and 5a (2 times)

G   C5   G   D5

Come on,   come on,   lov - in' for the mon-ey,   Come on,   come on,   lis -
                                    (Mon - ey   talks.)

ten to the mon-ey talk.   Come on,   come on,   lov - in' for the mon-ey.
(Mon - ey   talks.)   (Mon - ey

G   D5   To Coda

Come on,   come on,   lis -   ten to the mon-ey, talk.
talks.)   (Mon - ey

D5

                                    Mon - ey   talks.   Yeah! _____

lead guitar

with Rhythm figures 2 and 2a (2 times)

Yeah!

hold bend

D5

with Rhythm figure 3

C5

with Rhythm figure 4

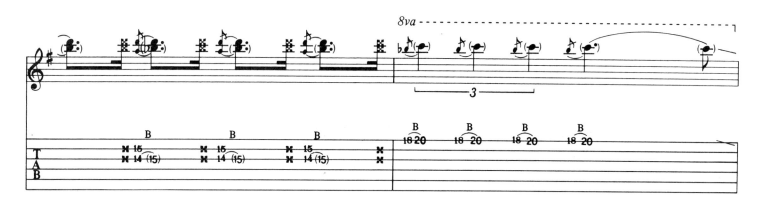

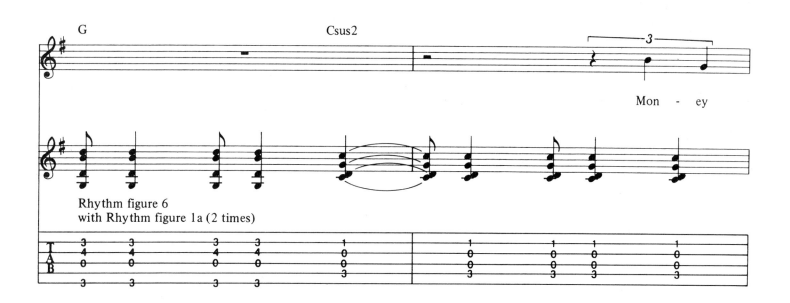

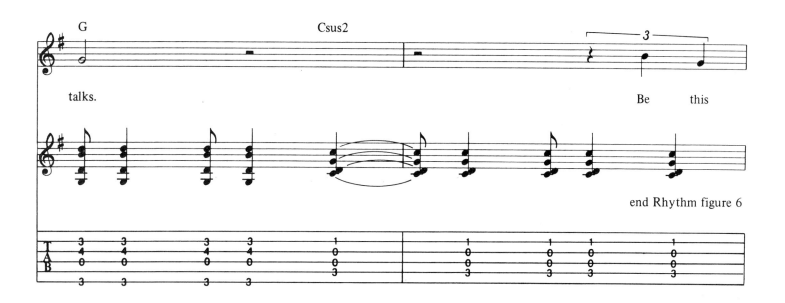

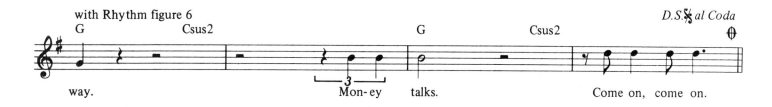

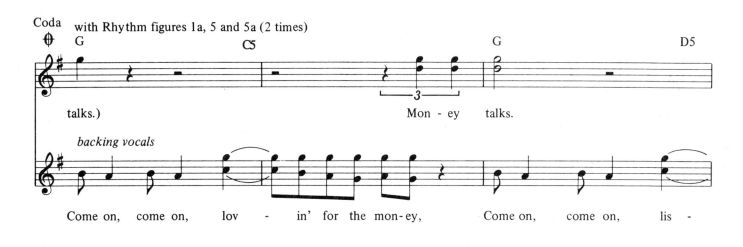

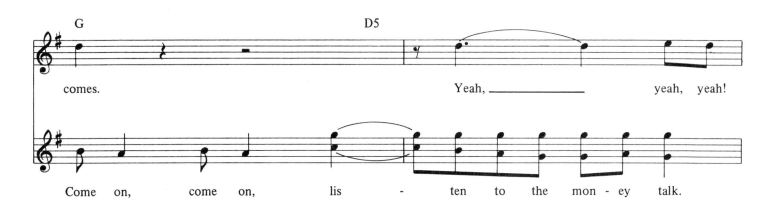

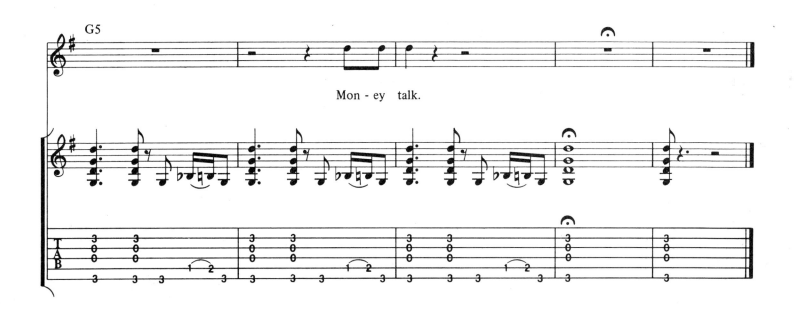